THE LIFE AND TIMES OF

MOTHER TERESA

Tanya Rice

CHELSEA HOUSE PUBLISHERS

Philadelphia

First published in traditional hardback edition
© 1998 by Chelsea House Publishers.
Printed in Hong Kong
Copyright © Parragon Book Service Ltd 1995
Unit 13–17, Avonbridge Trading Estate, Atlantic Road
Avonmouth, Bristol, England BS11 9QD

Cover picture and illustrations courtesy of Rex Features

Library of Congress Cataloging-in-Publication Data
Rice, Tanya.
    [Mother Teresa]
    The life and times of Mother Teresa / by Tanya Rice.
       p.   cm.
    Originally published: Mother Teresa. London : Parragon
Books, 1994.
    Includes index.
    Summary: A biography of the nun who founded the order
known as "The Congregation of the Missionaries of Charity" to
work with the sick and destitute in Calcutta and other places
and who was awarded the Nobel Peace Prize in 1979.
    ISBN 0-7910-4637-0 (hc)
    1. Teresa, Mother, 1910-   —Juvenile literature. 2. Nuns—
India—Calcutta—Biography—Juvenile literature. 3. Missionaries
of Charity—Biography—Juvenile literature. [1. Teresa, Mother,
1910-   . 2. Nuns. 3. Missionaries. 4. Missionaries of
Charity—Biography. 5. Missions—India. 6. Women—
Biography.] I. Title.
BX4406.5.Z8R53   1997
271'.97—dc21
    [B]   97-26030
                                                    CIP
                                                     AC

CONTENTS

Mother Teresa's motto

EARLY LIFE

A small, aged woman, wrapped in a simple white sari, moves between the beds, embracing the children. Their large, dark eyes shine out of frail faces. The utter poverty that has brought these children into her care is temporarily forgotten in her presence. She replaces deprivation with her love and, in accordance with her religion, with the love of God. Few people would fail to recognize this woman. She is Mother Teresa. Her only ambition has been to alleviate the suffering of the poorest of the poor, and for this she is renowned and respected around the world.

Christened Agnes Bojaxhiu, she was born on August 26, 1910, the youngest of Nikola and Drana's three children. Her sister, Aga, had been born in 1904, and her brother, Lazar, in 1907. They grew up together in the small Serbian town of Skopje, although the family was Albanian, living within Skopje's Albanian community. They had a pet name in their native language for their youngest member, "Gonxha," meaning "flower bud," because, as her brother Lazar once explained, she was pink and plump.

Agnes was born into unstable times; the first Albanian uprising occurred in 1910. Within two years the Balkan States would be at war, and this unrest would culminate in 1914 with the outbreak of the First World War. Luckily Agnes's father was a successful merchant and the family remained financially secure through this unsettling time. All three children attended the school that was attached to their local church. Then, when Agnes was only eight, her father suddenly died. Drana was grief-stricken for several months, but the needs of her children finally forced her to take control of the situation.

The daughter of a landowner and merchant, Drana was no stranger to hard work, and with admirable courage she quickly established her own business, selling embroidery and, later, the carpets for which Skopje was renowned. Inevitably Drana would be one of the deepest influences on her youngest daughter. As well as being strong and resourceful, Drana was a profoundly religious woman who led the family's recitation of the rosary every evening. The children called her "Nana Loke," meaning "Mother of My Soul," and grew used to welcoming strangers at the dinner table, because Drana made a habit of inviting the poorer members of their community to join the family at mealtimes. She also found waste of any kind intolerable; one evening, when the children were idly chatting, she turned the light out, telling them that it was a waste of electricity.

Religion played a part in almost every aspect of Agnes's life. As members of the predominantly Albanian parish of the Sacred Heart, her family's social as well as religious life revolved around the church, which was itself a focus for the Albanian community's customs and traditions. With her elder sister, Aga, Agnes attended Skopje's state secondary school, where she was by all accounts a good student, though Aga may have been the better scholar. The two girls spent a great deal of time together and shared a love of music. They both joined the church choir and the larger Albanian Catholic Choir. Their brother, Lazar, on the other hand, preferred sports and spent his free time with young men of his own age. He once recalled that he had a particular weakness for sweet things and would raid the pantry at night for treats. Agnes would remind him that he should not have any food after midnight if he was to attend mass in the morning, but she never told their mother of his lapses. In 1924 Lazar left home to join a military academy in Austria, leaving the family without any man to head it in the traditional sense. In 1925, however, Father Jambrenkoic of the Society of Jesus became the local pastor and he would guide young Agnes. At the age of twelve, she had already expressed a desire to become a nun.

Father Jambrenkoic set up a branch of the Sodality of the Blessed Virgin Mary for his younger parishioners. Originally established in 1563, the Sodality drew inspiration from St. Ignatius Loyola's questions: "What have I done for Christ? What am I doing for Christ? What will I do for Christ?" Agnes joined the group, which would provoke and stimulate her thoughts and feelings about God. The Sodality also focused on the lives of other saints and also of missionaries. Father Jambrenkoic was particularly enthusiastic about the missionary work of the Jesuits, and most especially about their work with the poor and with lepers. He told stories and read letters from Yugoslav priests who had gone to Bengal in 1924, some of whom were stationed in the outskirts of Calcutta. Agnes caught his enthusiasm and would help Father Jambrenkoic describe the missionaries' work to local people, drawing on a map to show where the missions were at the time. Agnes was also a member of a prayer group whose particular concern was praying for the church's missions in India. Their work inspired her so much that she asked her cousin, who taught mandolin, to give his earnings to her for the missions in India.

When Drana made her regular pilgrimage to the shrine of Our Lady of Cernagore in Letnice, in the mountains of Montenegro, she encouraged her daughters to accompany her. At this time Agnes's health needed extra care because she was prone to malaria and whooping cough, and the mountain air was therefore particularly good for her. Agnes loved to spend her spare time reading, but on these trips it

A Calcutta street in 1930

was her sister's particular responsibility to take Agnes on long walks and then make sure that she rested. In 1928, on the feast of the Assumption, the three women made their last visit to Letnice together. Agnes had spent six years trying to understand her wish to become a nun, wanting to be sure that it was the right decision. Father Jambrenkoic had told her that if she had a vocation she would feel an intense joy, joy at the thought of serving God. Finally, Agnes was sure that she was meant to be a nun, and furthermore, a missionary. After all she had read and heard about it, her heart was set on India, and in Letnice that year she knew that the time had come for her to follow her vocation. When Agnes told her mother, Drana stayed in her room for twenty-four hours; one can imagine how Drana struggled with herself, neither wanting to see another member of her family leave, nor wanting to deny the will of God. Finally she gave Agnes her blessing and offered her some advice: "Put your hand in His hand and walk all the way with Him." It was advice that Agnes would never forget.

Agnes applied to the Order of Loreto Nuns, whose work as missionaries in Bengal she had heard so much about. She was accepted and left Skopje on September 25, 1928. She had to go to Zagreb first to meet up with another novitiate, Betike Kanjc, so that they could make the next leg of their journey together. It was in Zagreb that Agnes said her final good-byes to the friends who had come to wish her well, and to her mother and sister, who had accompanied her. Agnes was only eighteen and, sad as she must have felt that day, she did not know that she would never see her mother again. The two young women had to undertake the difficult journey to Ireland and the Loreto Nuns' Mother House in Rathfarman. They were setting off for a new life and their apprehension must have been tinged with excitement.

The Loreto Order is the Irish branch of the Institute of the Blessed Virgin Mary and was founded in 1609 by Mary Ward, who was from Yorkshire, England. Her epitaph sums up her vocation: "To love the poor, preserve the same, live, die and rise with them, was all the aim of Mary Ward." Eventually, after a somewhat patchy history, the Order was asked to establish a post in Calcutta. It is easy to see what drew the young Agnes to them.

As a novitiate, Agnes spent six weeks learning English and getting her first real taste of what life would be like within the order she had chosen. She would complete her training as a novitiate in Darjeeling in India. On January 6, 1929, the Feast of Epiphany, she arrived in Calcutta, but this first visit would be brief as she still had to travel another 450 miles to reach her destination.

The British had used Darjeeling as a resting place for their troops in the mid-nineteenth century. Nestled in the foothills of the Himalayas and surrounded by tea plantations, it quickly became a popular hill station: a new road, a sanatorium, and a hotel were built. Darjeeling boomed and by 1857 this once-secluded spot had some 10,000 inhabitants; in the 1880s its famous mini-railway was completed. An enclave of the British Empire, it was far removed from the filth and poverty of Calcutta. Agnes's life behind the walls of the Loreto Convent in Darjeeling settled down into a routine of prayer, teaching, and receiving instructions from the novice mistress.

Nearly two and a half years after she arrived in India, Agnes took her first vows as a Sister of Loreto, on May 24, 1931. She chose to be named after her patron saint, St. Therese of Lisieux or St. Therese of the Child Jesus. Saint Therese died young of tuberculosis, but it was her love of missions and prayers for priests, especially missionaries, that had inspired the Pope to name her, and St. Francis Xavier, patron of all missions around the world. There was a complication, however: since another novice named Therese was already at the convent, Agnes adopted the Spanish spelling. She was now Sister Teresa.

Having served another six years as a novitiate, Sister

Teresa took her lifelong vows of poverty, chastity, and obedience on May 14, 1937. She was now ready to move on from Darjeeling. She was sent to the Loreto Convent in Entally, an eastern district of Calcutta. Here the Loreto Nuns had a large property called St. Mary's where they ran a girls' school for some five hundred pupils, mostly boarders who had been orphaned. In fact, the convent had originally been established as an orphanage for children of all denominations. A high wall surrounded the compound, which also included a smaller school attended by local Bengali girls, most of whom were middle class.

Far from home, Sister Teresa discovered an unexpected link to Skopje in St. Mary's School. Here there was an active branch of the same organization that had so influenced her own schoolgirl years, the Sodality of the Blessed Virgin. The members of this branch worked to relieve the terrible poverty of families living in the slum so near the convent. Their work was guided by Father Julien Henry, the priest at St. Teresa's. Every Saturday some of the girls would visit the slum while others went to the large Nilratan Sarkar Hospital with the aim of comforting the poor and the sick. Sister Teresa would encourage the girls' work, though she could not accompany them herself. Perhaps one person, her pupil Subashini Das, saw the potential that Sister Teresa had as a leader who might set an even more active example to the girls.

In order to teach at the schools, Sister Teresa had to learn Bengali, to which she would add Hindi, while she also became fluent in English. She taught geography and then history in both schools, and gave her full commitment to her religious life as part of the community she had joined. No one could have guessed at that time that the young Sister would one day give up this life and leave the convent. The plight of the very poor was never far from her thoughts, however, and the life of the convent was not so secluded that the Sisters never left its walls. Sister Teresa's teaching also took her to the local church's primary school, St. Teresa's. This meant leaving the clean and ordered life of the convent and walking through the poverty-stricken streets of the nearby slums. Before coming to Entally, the young Sister had never seen poverty like this.

By the early 1940s India was entering a period of turmoil as Britain slowly lost its grip on its empire. In 1943 India suffered a disastrous famine that cost at least two million lives, when boats used to transport rice were redeployed for the British war effort. As India found itself tragically drawn into a war it had nothing to do with, Gandhi's nonviolent resistance to British rule intensified. The uncertain times brought internal unrest between the Muslim and Hindu communities. August 16, 1946, was declared "Direct Action Day" by the Muslim League; in Calcutta, the head of the administration, who was Muslim, declared it a public holiday. The tension between Muslims and Hindus boiled over into terrible violence and the city was paralyzed. Later, Mother Teresa would recall, "I saw bodies on the streets, stabbed, beaten, lying there in dried blood." The following year would bring partition and India would finally be released from British rule, but not without massive disruption and still more violence. Sixteen million people were on the move as Hindus and Sikhs fled into India, while Muslims headed to Pakistan. Calcutta would become the new home of many displaced and desperately poor people.

It is against this background that Sister Teresa's early life as a nun must be seen. Though it would have been perfectly normal for her to stay at the convent for the rest of her life, these were not normal times and there was no telling what one might be called upon to do.

The only other regular excursion Sister Teresa would make outside the convent was an annual retreat to Darjeeling, where she would concentrate on deepening her religious commitment. On the train to Darjeeling for one such retreat, Sister Teresa experienced what she has since called "an inner command." It was September 10, 1946, nine and a half years after her move to Calcutta. She has described how God told her to renounce her life within the convent and go into the slums to work and live among the poorest of the poor. "The message was quite clear, it was an order. I was to leave the convent. I felt that God wanted something more from me. He wanted me to be poor and to love Him in the distressing disguise of the poorest of the poor." She felt the call all through her retreat and knew that she must answer it.

A small child finds comfort

SERVING THE POOREST OF THE POOR

When she first returned from Darjeeling, she went to seek the permission she would need in order to follow the direction of her new calling. She shared her thoughts with other Sisters and she sought the support of her superiors, including the Archbishop of Calcutta. Keeping her identity secret, the Archbishop discussed the matter with Father Henry and with Father Celeste van Exem, Sister Teresa's spiritual director. Father van Exem was a key figure in Sister Teresa's spiritual development and was one of the first to know of the "inner command" that was compelling her. He guided her in her dealings with the Archbishop of Calcutta and it was he who eventually told her that permission had been granted, that her prayers had been answered. When the time came, Sister Teresa asked him to bless a simple sari, the kind that every poor Bengali woman wore, and a small cross and rosary. These were the symbols she chose for her new role.

The Archbishop could see that the Daughters of St. Anne were already involved in the sort of work Sister Teresa had been called to do, and so he suggested that she join. However, it was their practice to return to the seclusion of the convent at the end of each day's work among the poor. Sister Teresa was clear that not only had she been called to work with the poor, but she was also to live among them. This complicated matters because Sister Teresa would have

Calcutta street children

to be released from the Loreto Order because no one within it was doing similar work. She was told to write to the Mother General of Loreto in Dublin and ask for her permission to leave the congregation. Sister Teresa's calling would now take her down one of two paths: she had either to ask her Mother General for secularization, which would mean she would no longer be a nun; or she could ask for exclaustration, which would enable her to leave her closed order, but still be bound by her vows of poverty, chastity, and obedience. If she were no longer a nun, it would be difficult, even impossible, to get others to join her and so begin a new religious community to fulfill the calling God had given her. For unknown reasons, it seems that the Archbishop told Sister Teresa that she must apply for secularization and, despite Father van Exem's intervention, insisted that she put her faith in God. When the Mother General's reply came, Sister Teresa had been granted exclaustration. One further hurdle remained: she now had to write to Rome and seek the same permission, and again the Archbishop insisted that she ask for secularization.

This final stage was neither easy nor speedy, and to Sister Teresa—so clear that God had called her not only to work, but also to live with the poor—the wait seemed endless. On August 7, 1948, the letter from Rome, dated April 12, finally arrived in Calcutta. Sister Teresa's prayers had been answered: she could leave the Loreto Order, but remain a nun. She would keep her vows of poverty and chastity, but, instead of being bound to the Loreto Order, she now owed her obedience to the Archbishop of Calcutta.

It was what she had wanted, what she knew God was calling her to do, yet leaving the convent at Entally and the community that had been so much a part of her life was one of the hardest things for Sister Teresa to sacrifice. "Loreto meant everything to me," she once said. On being given the news of Sister Teresa's mission, the other Sisters were told neither to question nor to praise her decision. She was on her own.

A sister feeds an orphan

MEDICAL TRAINING AND
A PLACE TO LIVE

The first thing Sister Teresa needed was some medical training, since there would be little hope of helping the "poorest
of the poor" without it. So when she left the Loreto Order in
her simple sari and sandals, she set off for Petna, a city on
the Ganges some 240 miles from Calcutta. Here the Medical
Mission Sisters would introduce Sister Teresa to some basic
medical skills. Sister Teresa always talked to the other
Sisters about the spiritual side of her new calling, in which
the time given to prayer, penance, and fasting would be as
important as the work she would carry out. Hearing this,
there was one thing that the Sisters stressed to Sister Teresa:
if she was to be of any use to the poor as God intended,
then she had an obligation to look after her own health. She
must not let her compassion for the poor lead her to neglect
her personal hygiene or the rest she would need in order to
work effectively, and she must maintain a healthy diet. She
could not, they told her, eat as little as the poor and expect
to keep her health. She would have to combine her spiritual
life with a practical approach if she wished to be of any
service to the poor.

After almost four months with the Medical Mission
Sisters, Sister Teresa was granted permission to return to
Calcutta, where Father van Exem had found her a place with

the Little Sisters of the Poor at their house for the elderly, the St. Joseph's home. Here she divided her time between looking after the home's elderly residents and visiting the poor in the *bustee,* or slum, at Motijhil, the workers' housing just outside the Loreto Convent in Entally. Simply by starting to write out the alphabet one day in the dirt, she managed to establish a school at Motijhil, the bustee she had only been able to look down on from the convent's windows. Before long there were donations of chairs and a blackboard, and eventually she was able to hire a couple of rooms for her small school. It was hard and lonely work, and Sister Teresa sometimes felt the pull of the familiarity and comforts of her old life at the convent. At such times she turned to God to give her the courage and strength she needed to continue with the work she knew she had been called to do.

The next step was for Sister Teresa to find a place where she could develop her work independently. She approached Father van Exem, who in turn sought the help of Michael Gomes, a Bengali Catholic who lived with his family in a large three-story house, 14 Creek Lane. Half of the house was empty and it was Michael's young daughter Mabel who suggested that Sister Teresa use the space to begin her work.

February 1949 found Sister Teresa moving into 14 Creek Lane with just one small suitcase. For a brief period Sister Teresa kept a journal recording her work, and the entry she made on that first night at Creek Lane reveals how hard it was for her at the beginning:

28 February
Today, my God, what tortures of loneliness. I wonder how long my heart will suffer this. Tears rolled and rolled. Everyone sees my weakness. My God give me courage.

Her room was furnished with only a packing case (which would serve as her desk), one chair, and some other wooden boxes that would be put to use as seats. One other person came with her, Charur Ma, who had been the cook at St. Mary's. The two of them shopped for the supplies the bustee school needed. Michael Gomez accompanied them whenever possible, begging for medical supplies for the dispensary Sister Teresa was determined to establish.

The house at 14 Creek Lane quickly attracted those who wished to join Sister Teresa in her work. On March 19, 1949, Subashini Das, her former pupil and a boarder at St. Mary's since she was nine, followed Sister Teresa's example, as she had predicted she might. She turned up at Creek Lane and asked if she could assist Sister Teresa in her work among the poor. Only a few weeks later, Magdalena Gomes, another old pupil, also joined them. Their number quickly swelled to ten within only a few months, although two decided to leave, having put their vocation to the test and finding that they were not right for the work.

The Missionaries of Charity

THE MISSIONARIES OF CHARITY

After a year, Sister Teresa's position had to be reviewed. She had taken Indian citizenship during that year, and she made it quite clear that she had no intention of leaving. The Archbishop of Calcutta saw that the best thing to do would be to formalize the intentions and rules for Sister Teresa's burgeoning new community. He would apply to the office of the Propagation of the Faith in Rome to have the work of Sister Teresa and her followers recognized as a congregation of his archdiocese. The first step was to draw up a constitution that would guide the Sisters. The new congregation would be called the Missionaries of Charity. In addition to the vows of poverty, chastity, and obedience, there would be a fourth vow, which would serve to direct their work: "to give whole-hearted and free service to the poorest of the poor."

On October 7, 1950, a mass was held to celebrate the inauguration of the new congregation and Father van Exem read out the decree of recognition:

To fulfill our mission of compassion and love, to the poorest of the poor we go—seeking out in towns and villages all over the world, even amid squalid surroundings, the poorest, the abandoned, the sick, the infirm, the leprosy patients, the dying, the desperate, the lost, the outcast, taking care of them, rendering help to them, visiting them assiduously, living Christ's love for them, and awakening their response to His great love.

The founder of the Missionaries of Charity was also recognized with a new title: Sister Teresa was now Mother Teresa. Subashini Das would become Sister Agnes, and Magdalena Gomes became Sister Gertrude.

Within three years, the community had outgrown 14 Creek Lane, and in February 1953 the diocese bought 54a Lower Circular Road. Father van Exem used his contacts in the city and the property was bought from a Muslim family who were moving to Dhaka (in Bangladesh), at a price that barely covered the value of the land the house stood on. This location thus became the Mother House of the Missionaries of Charity, where it remains to this day. The additional space meant that a chapel could be established, giving a new focus to the Sisters' work with the poor, sick, homeless, and dying. From their new Mother House, the Sisters' difficult work continued.

Dressed in saris, the women sought out the poorest areas of Calcutta, where they found young children in desperate need of special care and where they tried to help anyone who was dying, whether in the gutters of busy streets or hidden away in alleyways. Hindus consider death to involve elements of impurity, and Hindu landlords disliked people dying in their accommodations. Likewise, rickshaw and taxi drivers might avoid taking seriously ill passengers. Worse still, hospitals were reluctant to admit patients for whom they could do nothing. The sight of the dead and the dying abandoned in the streets presented Mother Teresa with a clear priority. She must establish a home for the dying, somewhere these people would always be accepted and welcomed.

With a directness and humility that would characterize all her dealings with officialdom, Mother Teresa approached the Commissioner of Police and the Health Officer of Calcutta and asked for their help in finding a suitable place where the destitute might be allowed to die with dignity. She was given a simple pilgrims' hostel, Nirmal Hriday, near the temple of

The Life and Times of

Kalie in Kalighat. Named after the powerful Hindu goddess Kali, Kalighat is still one of the most overcrowded parts of south Calcutta. Her ancient temple stands on the banks of a tributary to the Ganges, sacred river of the Hindus. The pilgrims' hostel was exactly what Mother Teresa needed: it had gas, electricity, and lots of space. But it was filthy, so the Sisters' first job was to clean the entire building. Then they set about their real task of giving a home to the dying.

While all holy people are treated with respect in India—so much so that none of Mother Teresa's followers ever encountered danger from violence—some locals were unhappy about a Christian group working in such close proximity to a holy Hindu temple. Malicious rumors began to spread that the dying were being ministered the last rites and given Christian burials against their will. Dr. Ahmad, the Chief Medical Officer, and a senior police official decided to visit Nirmal Hriday themselves. They saw Mother Teresa hunched over a figure whose face was little more than a terrible wound. Unobserved, they watched as Mother Teresa used tweezers to remove maggots from this wound, the smell of which would have been enough to keep most people from even entering the room. They heard Mother Teresa comforting the disfigured patient. She asked the patient to say a prayer to his god, while she would say one to hers.

Word had spread of the officials' visit to Nirmal Hriday and a crowd had gathered outside. The police officer told them that he would send Mother Teresa away only when they and their sisters and mothers came to do the work instead.

Despite the officials' clear support, tension in the local community continued. One day a young temple priest was discovered to be dying of tuberculosis. There was no hope of a cure for him and the hospitals refused to give a bed to a hopeless case. He found himself in Nirmal Hriday, where Mother Teresa cared for him until he died. The other priests could not fail to notice the compassion she had shown, nor

Doing the washing at Nirmal Hriday

did they overlook the fact that Mother Teresa sent his body to be cremated according to the Hindu rites. Given this example of her work, all resentment and hostility faded away.

The Missionaries of Charity's declared aim is to give the love they find in God to those they care for and attend to. Many have criticized Mother Teresa, believing that she forces her own religious creed upon people who are at their most vulnerable. Author and feminist Germaine Greer wrote in the *Independent* on September 22, 1990, "Mother Teresa epitomized for me the blinkered charitableness upon which we pride ourselves and for which we expect reward in this world and the next." Mother Teresa has clearly stated, however, that neither she nor any Missionary of Charity seeks converts. Only those who request it are given a Christian burial; to do otherwise would be considered a sacrilege by the Missionaries of Charity. Where medical science can do no more, Mother Teresa offers love and care to those who are abandoned by every member of their society, and ensures that they do not die alone.

The overwhelming impression of those who have sought to understand Mother Teresa is that her love of God motivates her every action. According to her faith, each body that she nurses is the body of Christ, and in loving those who come into her care she is loving Christ.

It was inevitable that Mother Teresa would identify another major group in Indian society who were abandoned and made outcasts through no fault of their own: lepers. No matter what their background, people with leprosy would leave their families so as not to bring disgrace to them or have them suffer in any way. While subsistence could be made by begging at the beginning, the progression of the disease caused loss of feeling and susceptibility to further infection and loss of limb. Having tried and failed to set up a leprosy clinic when the only hospital to treat leprosy in the vast

Inside Nirmal Hriday

sprawl of Calcutta was closed after the uncharitable objections of locals and property developers, Mother Teresa could only turn to prayer.

One day an ambulance was donated to the Missionaries and Mother Teresa saw that it could be transformed into a mobile clinic for leprosy. At the same time Dr. Sen, a skin and leprosy specialist, offered his services to Mother Teresa for free. To Mother Teresa, it was the answer to her prayers. In September 1957, the first mobile leprosy clinic was launched. Dr. Sen treated the lepers, but also trained the Sisters in this specialized work. It was the first of many clinics that would work by going to sites where lepers were known to gather and then returning a week later, treating the lepers and keeping meticulous records. If patients went missing one week, the Sisters would search the area until they were found, to be sure they were not in distress.

Mother Teresa also realized that she would have to fight against the ignorance that caused these people to be made outcasts. She increased the awareness of the needs of lepers, and groups began to appear collecting donations to help the lepers. Not only did people begin to understand that lepers could be helped, but the lepers themselves began to feel that they were not being abandoned altogether. Eventually, in 1969, the attitude toward lepers had changed so much that the government felt able to give an area of thirty-six acres to the Missionaries so that a town could be built as a home for the lepers. Mother Teresa called it Shanti Nagar ("Town of Peace") because here the lepers could truly live in peace, without the fear of being moved on. They could also be offered treatment, and for those who could be cured, help was offered with rehabilitation so that they could return as full members of the wider community.

Children have always been of key importance to Mother Teresa as she has pursued her vocation. As the Missionaries of Charity grew and new convents were established, both in India and in other parts of the world, the Sisters also tried to

The Children's Home of the Immaculate

open children's homes nearby. Called Shishu Bhawan, these centers house children ranging in age from the tiniest infants to seven-year-olds. Apart from some of the younger children, they are educated at local schools. Any expenses, whether for uniforms or books, are met by the Missionaries of Charity. Perhaps most well known of all the many children's homes is Nirmala Shishu Bhavan, the Children's Home of the Immaculate, which is on Lower Circular Road, a short walk from the Mother House.

Many have reported how they visited Nirmala Shishu Bhavan expecting to find the atmosphere heavy with the children's feelings of abandonment. Here are children who have been plucked from pavements, out of trash cans, or from the arms of policemen who have found them on their doorsteps. There are also children from the Calcutta hospitals, where Mother Teresa has told doctors that she will take any and all unwanted babies, saying, "I'm fighting abortion with adoption." Many of the children are sick and some of them are terminally ill, but in Nirmala Shishu Bhavan all of them are cared for and loved by the Sisters.

Mother Teresa has tried particularly hard to establish Shishu Bhawans at each of the leprosy centers so that parents with leprosy can pass their children into the care of the Sisters. Parents are still able to visit their children, but are discouraged from touching or kissing them, to prevent exposure to the risk of infection.

Over the years, the Missionaries of Charity have spread all over the world to form a network of schools, dispensaries, homes for abandoned children and for leprosy sufferers, for alcoholics and for drug addicts, for the destitute and the dying. More recently they have also established centers for those with AIDS. Today there are some five hundred Missionaries of Charity centers around the world. For the first ten years, and in accordance with the regulations of the Roman Catholic Church, the Missionaries of Charity did not take their work beyond Calcutta. Mother Teresa was

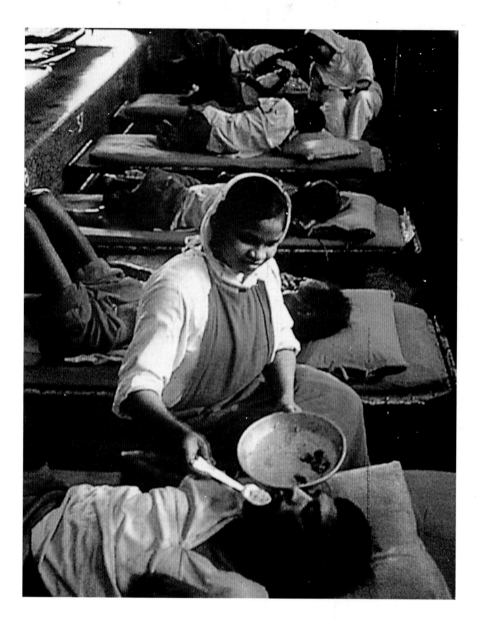

Sisters feed the sick at Nirmal Hriday

reportedly impatient with this restriction, but the Arch-bishop of Calcutta, ever cautious, would not bend the rules for her.

In 1960 she was allowed to open her first center outside Calcutta, which she promptly did in a town called Ranchi. The next was in Delhi and Prime Minister Jawaharlal Nehru opened it even though he was unwell at the time. When Mother Teresa asked him if she could tell him about the work of the Missionaries, he answered, "No, Mother, you do no need to tell me about your work. I already know about it, that is why I am here." In 1962 she was the first person who was not Indian by birth to receive the prestigious Padma Shri award from the president of India. Nehru had commended her for it.

Once it was made possible, expansion was rapid. Twenty-five centers were open in India by the end of the 1960s, eighty-six by the end of the 1980s, and now there are nearly two hundred. The first house to be opened outside India was in Venezuela in 1965. The Papal Nuncio in New Delhi, Archbishop Knox, thought that the Missionaries of Charity were needed in Venezuela. While the Archbishop of Calcutta had been reluctant to let Mother Teresa's community grow too rapidly, he could not stand in the way of the Papal Nuncio. It is interesting to note that in February 1965 the Missionaries of Charity became a congregation of pontifical right, which meant that they were no longer answerable to the Archbishop of Calcutta, but to the Vatican. Mother Teresa was invited by the Bishop of Venezuela to assess the situation herself, and this became the pattern for the opening of all new centers: the local bishop would invite Mother Teresa and she would visit the country herself. She was going to be very busy.

In 1968 the second overseas house was opened in Rome; in 1969 two were established in Australia. Four more were added in 1970, one each in London and Jordan, and another two in Venezuela. Then came New York, Bangladesh, Northern Ireland, the Gaza Strip, Yemen, Ethiopia, Sicily, Papua New

Guinea, the Philippines, Panama, Japan, Portugal, Brazil, and Burundi. More houses have opened in Britain and America, and they can now be found in the former Soviet Union, in South Africa, and all over Eastern Europe, including Mother Teresa's home country of Albania. At each of these centers, the work has been carried out by an ever-expanding number of missionaries. Naturally many have wished to test their vocation, and training centers for novitiates have sprung up alongside work centers.

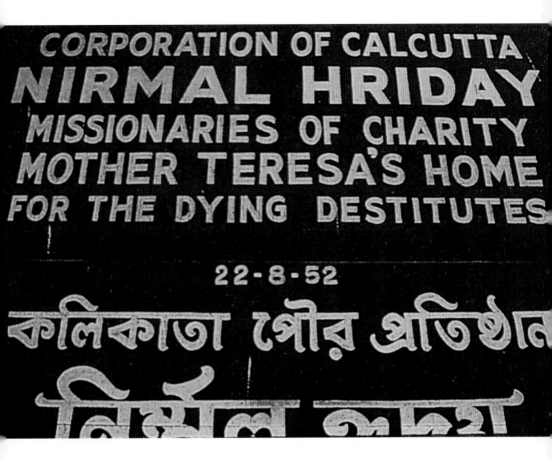

Entrance to the Home for the Dying

Mother Teresa

THE CHARITY BROTHERS AND
THE CO-WORKERS GROUPS

Men have also been inspired to join Mother Teresa. In 1963 the Missionaries of Charity Brothers was founded. Mother Teresa had called on Father van Exem in 1961 to ask for his help with a particular matter. It had become obvious that the help of some men might be useful in the supervision of the older boys and with some of the heavier work. She asked Father van Exem if he could help her to find some suitable candidates. In due course, some Brothers were sent to Calcutta and were housed at Shishu Bhawan, but it became apparent that the Brothers needed a different environment. More critically, some were reluctant to join because the Brothers were not officially recognized by the Roman Catholic Church. The spiritual guidance of the Brothers was being shared between Father Henry and Mother Teresa, but this was unsatisfactory in the long term because the Roman Catholic Church does not allow women to head male communities.

Mother Teresa began to search for a priest who would lead the Brothers. Father Ian Travers-Ball, a Jesuit priest, arrived in Shishu Bhavan, where he knew Mother Teresa was guiding a group of young men, intending to stay a month or so to learn what he could. A tall, charismatic, articulate man, he had arrived in India from Australia in 1954 and become interested in the poor while working in the mining district of Hazaribagh. Finding that the work being done at Shishu Bhavan moved him deeply and realizing that the community was in need of a priest, Father Travers-Ball accepted Mother Teresa's invitation to stay on as the Brothers' priest when his month ended. The arrangement was provisional, because he had to seek the permission of his Jesuit superiors in order to take up the position. At last a letter arrived from the Society of Jesus in Rome in January 1966, granting him three options. He chose the third, which meant leaving the Society of Jesus (as Mother Teresa had left the Sisters of Loreto) and joining the Missionaries of Charity Brothers. He chose the title of General Servant for his new role as head of the male congregation, and took the religious name of Father Andrew.

Over the years, the work of the Brothers has developed in subtly different ways from that of the Sisters, although it is all done in the same spirit. The Brothers are less regimented and enclosed than the women, and have needed to adapt themselves more closely to the varied cultures in which they have found themselves working. The first overseas house the Brothers established was in war-ravaged Vietnam in the 1970s, where the Sisters did not have a presence. This has become their pattern: in cities and countries where the Sisters have not yet established themselves, the Brothers have set to work. In Los Angeles, Hong Kong, Japan, Taiwan, Korea, Guatemala, the Philippines, El Salvador, the Dominican Republic, Brazil, and Madagascar, they have taken up the tasks they could best perform: establishing shelters for homeless boys, alcoholics, and drug addicts.

It may seem that whatever Mother Teresa needed to continue her work would eventually present itself. On the other hand, she has also known how to absorb every available offer of help and has been able to put those offers to the best possible use. In 1954 Ann Blaikie, the wife of a British business-man working in India, offered to make toys that Christmas for the children in Mother Teresa's care. Toys were not needed as badly as clothes and Mother Teresa asked Ann to turn her skills to this end instead.

She took Ann to Nirmal Hriday, the Home for the Dying in Kalighat, and by the end of the day Ann Blaikie had changed from a well-meaning housewife to the woman who would establish the first Co-Workers group in Calcutta. She gathered together a group of women to make the clothes that were needed for that Christmas. They were duly thanked by Mother Teresa, who then pointed out to them that the two big festivals of the Hindu and Muslim calenders were fast approaching and that the other children were now looking forward to their new clothes as well. The work would have to go on.

When she returned to Britain Ann discovered others who had come into contact with Mother Teresa and wanted to continue to help her, and the Co-Workers spread to Britain as well. Wherever a new center has opened, Co-Workers appear too. Though their exact numbers are unknown, it is estimated that Britain has more than thirty thousand and the United States some ten thousand, which gives an indication of the size of this vast network of helpers.

Pope John Paul II visits Calcutta

THE MISSION CONTINUES

The woman who started her mission with only five rupees to her name never involved herself or her fellow Sisters in fund-raising. When she first began her work in Motijhil bustee, she would visit the local priests and beg for donations that would allow her to continue her work; some were generous, others were critical and unhelpful. These people might be forgiven for their mixed reactions to her pleas, for this European woman in the cheapest kind of sari, with a small cloth bag slung over her shoulder and sturdy sandals on her feet was hardly conventional; she did not even look like a nun anymore. However, although she met with some resistance at first, many were unflinching in their support.

She continued to work in the complete faith that God would provide whatever was needed, and even more deep-seated was her belief that she did not really need anything to answer God's call. On the other hand, just as she never turned away those who wished to help, she never refused a gift that could be made to serve the Missionaries' work. When Pope Paul VI visited Bombay in 1965, he gave Mother Teresa a white Cadillac that had been a gift to him. Unlike the old ambulance that had become her first mobile leprosy clinic, Mother Teresa could find no practical use for the ostentatious car. So she raffled it and raised some money for use in her work.

In much the same spirit, she avoided all attempts to glorify her role in the work of the Missionaries. When people asked her about her past and about the early influences on her life, she was always reticent and only became animated when the conversation turned to the work of her community. For many, though, Mother Teresa was inseparable from any of the work of the Missionaries. The most striking illustration of this was that despite Mother Teresa's own wish to resign as Superior of her order, her followers persistently refused to let her step down. Even after she was seriously ill and had sought permission to convene a special General Chapter in September 1990 so that a successor could be appointed, her Sisters voted unanimously to retain her as their Superior.

There can be no doubt that her work has had a profound effect on many people around the world, even on those in the highest positions of society and government. In 1980, for example, Britain's Prince Charles made a special journey to visit her mission in Calcutta during his tour of India. He would have met her again with Princess Diana in 1992, except that she was in poor health. When Princess Diana returned to Britain, she went to Rome where Mother Teresa was convalescing. These two women, who led such different lives, spent some time together in conversation and prayer. Mother Teresa did not just wait to be visited when Pope John Paul II asked her to be his envoy to Lebanon in 1982; she rescued 37 mentally handicapped children from a hospital that had been bombed during the war. She has also been forthright in her criticism: she drew the attention of the British Prime Minister Margaret Thatcher to Britain's acute housing problems. When the Gulf War began, she pleaded with President George Bush and Iraq's president, Saddam Hussein, to end the hostilities before many innocent lives were ruined. As soon as the war was over, she got the Iraqi president's permission to open half a dozen centers in the war-torn country so that she could begin to put right the

Mother Teresa is visited by Queen Elizabeth

Mother Teresa receives the Nobel Peace Prize

damage caused by the conflict.

Many countries and organizations recognized her work by awarding her their most prestigious prizes. One that captured every headline around the world was the Nobel Peace Prize, which she received in 1979. The money that so often accompanies these prizes has all contributed to the work of the Missionaries.

Until her death in 1997, Mother Teresa continued to fulfill her own part in that work, spending as much as half the year traveling to visit centers around the world. Her business card, which she gave to anyone who would take it, read:

> The fruit of Silence is Prayer
> The fruit of Prayer is Faith
> The fruit of Faith is Love
> The fruit of Love is Service
> The fruit of Service is Peace.

After fighting poor health for several years, Mother Teresa died of cardiac arrest on September 5, 1997 in the Missionaries' Calcutta headquarters. Millions of people all over the world mourned the loss of this remarkable woman, who was a shining example of goodness and love all her life.

INDEX

INDEX

Early morning mass at Nirmal Hriday